THE EXCRETORY SYSTEM

How Living Creatures
Get Rid of Wastes

Dr. Alvin Silverstein
and
Virginia B. Silverstein

Illustrated by Lee J. Ames

PRENTICE-HALL, INC., Englewood Cliffs, N.J.

The Excretory System: How Living Creatures
Get Rid of Wastes by Alvin Silverstein and
Virginia B. Silverstein

Printed in the United States of America   J

Prentice-Hall International, Inc., London
Prentice-Hall of Australia, Pty. Ltd., North Sydney
Prentice-Hall of Canada, Ltd., Toronto
Prentice-Hall of India Private Ltd., New Delhi
Prentice-Hall of Japan, Inc., Tokyo

10   9   8   7   6   5   4   3

Library of Congress Cataloging in Publication Data

Silverstein, Alvin.
    The excretory system.

    SUMMARY: Describes the construction and functions
of the various organs of the excretory system.
    1.   Excretion—Juvenile literature.   [1.]   Excretory
system]   I.   Silverstein, Virginia B., joint author.
II.   Ames, Lee J., illus.   III.   Title.
QP159.S54   574.1'4   72–4190
ISBN   0–13–293654–2

For Bessie Gurwitz

Contents

1
Wastes in Our World

One of the greatest problems in today's world is pollution. Smokestacks belch soot and poisonous gases out into the air. Millions of cars add more than their share of pollutants. The water of rivers and streams is fouled by solid and liquid wastes from industry and cities. Even the ocean is being covered by a layer of oil and various throwaway products of man's civilization.

Our bodies, too, are in constant danger of becoming polluted. Trillions of cells are working all the time producing wastes, which the cells dump into the rivers of the bloodstream. If these waste products are allowed to build up, the body will become poisoned, and die.

Fortunately, the body has a very efficient system for getting rid of wastes. This is the *excretory system.* It is a complicated system. Its parts are found throughout the body.

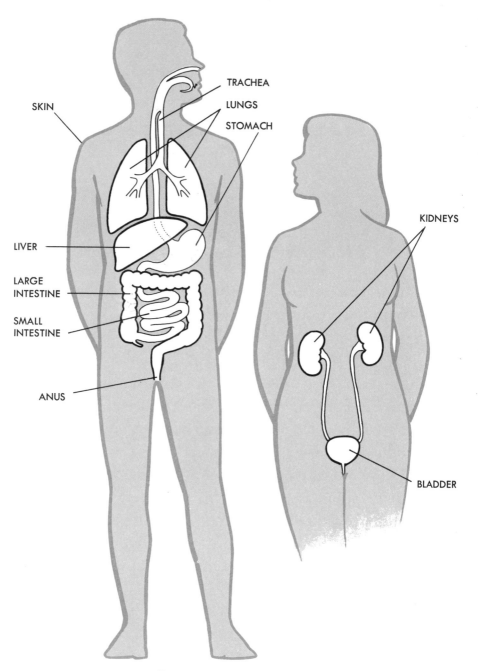

SKIN

TRACHEA

LUNGS

STOMACH

LIVER

LARGE
INTESTINE

SMALL
INTESTINE

ANUS

KIDNEYS

BLADDER

The Excretory System.

The skin that covers us gets rid of water and some solid wastes. Touch the inside of your palm. Does it feel moist? (If it does not, try jumping up and down for a minute and then touch your palm again.) The *sweat glands* pour waste materials out through tiny holes in the skin called *pores* (PORZ).

Your lungs also help to get rid of wastes. Place a small mirror in front of your mouth and breathe out. Notice the fog on the mirror. This is water vapor, which came out of your lungs. The lungs also give off another waste product that you cannot see: the gas *carbon dioxide.*

When you go to the bathroom, you can get rid of two different kinds of wastes. The solid wastes that come from undigested foods are called *feces* (FEE-SEEZ). One quarter or more of the feces are the bodies of bacteria that live in the intestines. The brown color of the feces comes from a chemical that is made out of dead red blood cells and excreted by the liver.

The liver is one of the busiest organs in the body. It performs more than two hundred different tasks. We could not live long without a liver. One of its most important jobs is to clear the body of poisons. It changes these poisons to other chemicals that are not harmful. Some of these may pass out in the feces. Others leave through the

3

most important clearinghouse of the body: the kidneys.

The kidneys are marvelous organs. They work furiously every minute of our lives. All the blood in the body flows through them many times each day. They work like miniature filters, and they produce the yellow fluid that we call *urine*.

All these parts of the excretory system are working within us whether we are awake or asleep, resting or active. They help to keep our bodies clean and healthy.

Every living organism has its own problems of waste disposal. Each manages to do a far more efficient job than man is doing in the technological world of today.

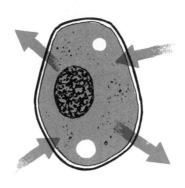

2
How Wastes Are Formed

Every living cell of the body is like a bustling factory. Thousands of different chemical reactions are going on at the same time. Some food materials are burned for energy. Others are broken down and built up into new chemicals.

Many of these body reactions give waste products, which must be disposed of. For example, crumple a small sheet of paper and place it in a glass or metal ashtray. Light it with a match, and let it burn until the flame goes out by itself. What is left in the ashtray when the burning is finished? Cautiously feel the outside of the ashtray. Burning produces heat, too.

When you burn paper, chemicals in the paper combine with *oxygen* of the air. Chemical bonds are broken, and the energy stored in them is released in the heat and light of the flame. The chemicals in paper are composed mainly of the elements *carbon, hydrogen,* and *oxygen.* Some of the carbon combines with oxygen to form *carbon monoxide* and carbon dioxide. These are gases that go off into the air. The burning reactions in the ashtray are not very efficient, and some of the carbon is left behind as black soot. The hydrogen and oxygen together form water. The burning paper is so hot that the water is in a gas form, and goes off into the air. That is why you do not see any water droplets in a flame. There are some salts and minerals in paper, and these do not burn. They form a grayish ash that is left behind in the ash-tray.

The body cells get energy by combining organic materials with oxygen (*oxidizing* them), but they do it much more efficiently than a fire. The chemical bonds are broken one at a time, and most of their energy is quickly captured and stored in new chemical bonds. Some energy is given off as heat, which must be removed from the cells. The cells of the body can oxidize the carbon of organic materials completely. No soot is left behind, because all the carbon atoms form carbon dioxide. Too much carbon dioxide can poison cells, and so this gas is one of the most important waste products of the body.

Many of the organic chemicals of the body also contain the element *nitrogen*. Nitrogen is a key part of the *amino* (A-MEEN-oh) group that gives *amino acids* their name. Amino acids are the build-

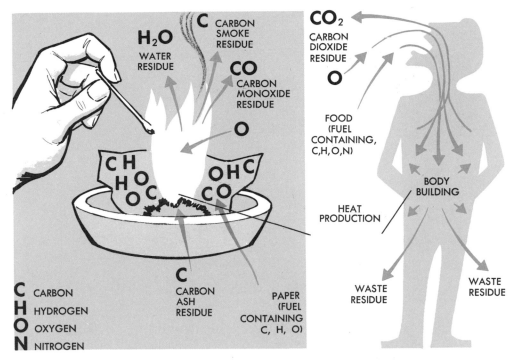

The body burns some food materials for energy and uses some as building blocks. Waste products are produced in both cases.

ing blocks of *proteins*. Proteins form the basic structures of the body. *Enzymes* (EN-zymz), chemicals that help other chemicals to react, are also proteins. When amino acids and other nitrogen compounds are changed in chemical reactions in the cells, some of the nitrogen may be released in the form of the compound *ammonia* (AM-MOHN-yuh).

Does your mother have a bottle of household cleaner containing ammonia? Remove the cap. Holding the bottle a few inches away from your

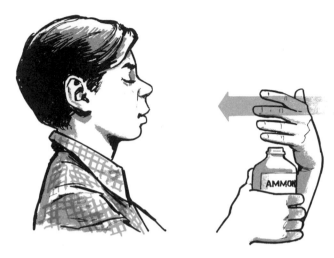

Be careful when sniffing ammonia!

face, wave your hand over the open top so that the fumes from the bottle are carried toward your nose. BE CAREFUL! Don't sniff too hard, and don't breathe in directly from the bottle. Even with these precautions, you will find that ammonia is a bad-smelling, irritating gas. It may make your eyes water, and your nose and throat may itch and burn.

Inside a cell, ammonia can be even worse. Too much ammonia is a poison that can kill a cell. One of the most important jobs of the excretory system is to change ammonia into other nitrogen compounds that are less poisonous, and to remove them from the body.

You don't usually think of water as a waste product. In fact, you should drink water every day, for your body needs it to live. Yet water is also produced in many of the chemical reactions of the body, both the "burning" reactions and the building reactions. Too much water can create problems in the body. It changes the concentrations of the chemicals in the blood and cells, and these chemicals must be in just the right concentrations to work properly. With too much water in the body, fluids build up in the cells and the spaces between them, and make the arms and legs and face puffy and sore.

Your excretory system gets rid of a quart of water or more each day. This is only part of the amazing juggling act that helps to keep all the systems of the body in balance.

3

The Human Kidney System

Fill a rubber balloon with water. From a small, wrinkled structure, it grows large and round and firm. If you wrap a rubber band around the neck, you can turn it with the neck down, and the water will still stay inside. But as soon as you loosen the rubber band, the water will come rushing out.

One of the structures of your excretory system is very much like a balloon. This is the *urinary* (YURE-ih-nery) *bladder.* Urine, the main liquid waste of the body, is stored in the bladder until you are ready to eliminate it. Your bladder can hold nearly a cup of water.

The bladder is found in the middle of your lower abdomen. When your bladder is full, and you feel that you have to go to the bathroom, it may feel painful if you press in on the front of your lower abdomen.

The walls of the bladder contain thick muscles, which can contract to help empty it. Just as you

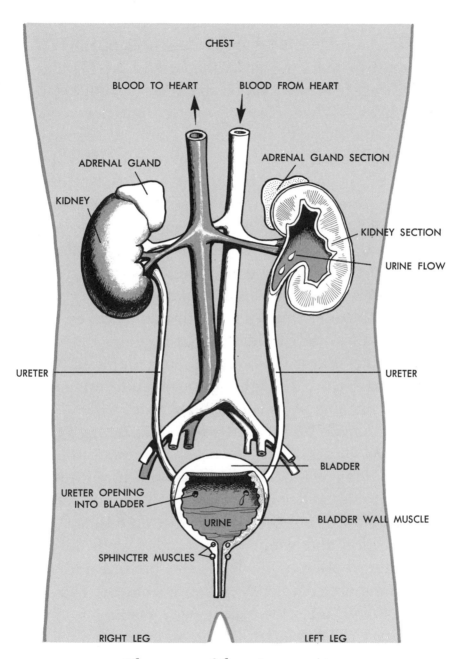

CHEST

BLOOD TO HEART   BLOOD FROM HEART

ADRENAL GLAND   ADRENAL GLAND SECTION

KIDNEY

KIDNEY SECTION

URINE FLOW

URETER   URETER

BLADDER

URETER OPENING
INTO BLADDER

URINE   BLADDER WALL MUSCLE

SPHINCTER MUSCLES

RIGHT LEG   LEFT LEG

The organs of the urinary tract.

placed a rubber band around the neck of the balloon to keep the water in, the neck of the bladder has rings of muscles called *sphincter* (SFING-TER) *muscles.* When the sphincter muscles contract, the ring gets smaller and closes off the neck of the bladder. When the sphincter muscles relax, the neck of the bladder is opened, and the urine stored in it can flow out. When you feel a need to urinate at an inconvenient time—when you are busy playing or in class in the middle of an important lesson—you squeeze hard on your sphincter muscles to hold the urine in.

The bladder empties into a thick tube called the *urethra* (YEW-REE-THRUH). Urine flows through this tube, out of the body. In boys and men, the urethra passes through the penis and ends in a small opening at its tip. *Seminal fluid,* which carries the male sex cells, also flows out through the urethra. But this fluid reaches the urethra through tubes that join it below the bladder. It never mixes with urine, and indeed, urine and seminal fluid never flow out of the body at the same time.

In girls and women, the urethra ends in an opening between the legs. The urethra and its opening are completely separate from the *vagina* (VA-GYNE-UH), the passageway leading to the *uterus* (YEW-TER-US), the organ in which a baby develops before birth.

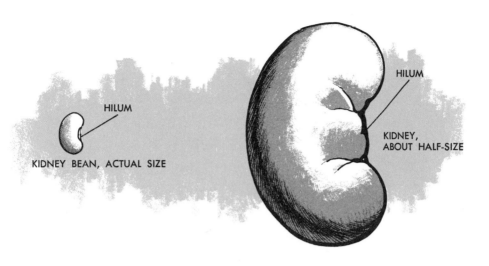

HILUM

KIDNEY BEAN, ACTUAL SIZE

HILUM

KIDNEY, ABOUT HALF-SIZE

The kidney bean is shaped like a kidney.

When you filled the balloon with water, you filled it through the neck. The bladder does not fill up in this way. Urine continually trickles into it through two narrow tubes which join it in the rounded part. These tubes are called *ureters* (YEW-REE-TERZ). They lead down to the bladder from the kidneys, where urine is formed. Valves, which can close like the shutter of a camera, keep urine from being forced back toward the kidneys when the bladder contracts.

Have you ever eaten kidney beans? They are named after the kidneys, because they are shaped like miniature kidneys. The kidneys are found just inside the rear wall of the body, at about the level of the waist. One is on each side of the spinal column. The organs of the body are all packed

13

neatly together like the pieces of a three-dimensional jigsaw puzzle, with no space wasted. The liver is packed in above the kidneys, and because this large organ is mainly on the right side of the body, the right kidney is slightly lower than the left.

When two prizefighters are in a clinch, you may notice one of them hitting at the other's lower back with his gloves. These jabs are called kidney punches, and they are illegal because they may cause serious damage to the kidneys. The kidneys are protected from most injuries by a pad of fat an inch thick, which surrounds them.

If you look closely at a kidney bean, you will see that one side curves outward, while the opposite side curves inward. In the middle of the hollow there is a little scar, where the bean came off its stalk in the seed pod. This scar is called the *hilum* (HYE-lum). If the seed were allowed to sprout, the first tiny root would poke its tip out through a tiny hole at one end of the hilum.

The hilum is an important part of your kidney, too. Nerves and blood vessels enter the kidney through this notched-in region. The rest of the organ is surrounded by a smooth, white cover.

If your mother has ever served kidneys for dinner, you may know that these organs are a rich red color. That is because they have an unusually

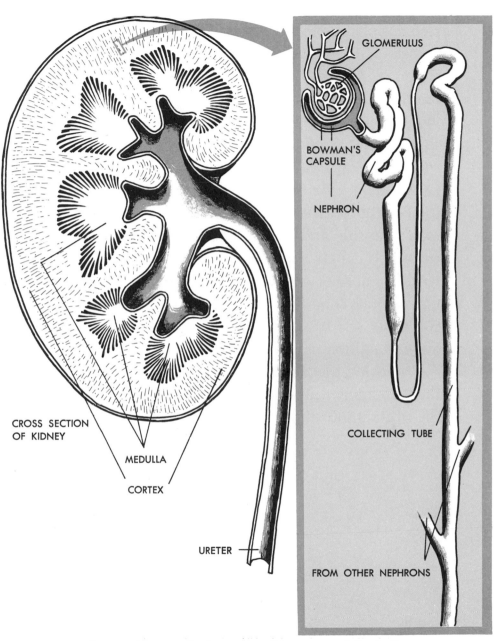

CROSS SECTION
OF KIDNEY

MEDULLA

CORTEX

URETER

GLOMERULUS

BOWMAN'S
CAPSULE

NEPHRON

COLLECTING TUBE

FROM OTHER NEPHRONS

The nephron is the basic working unit of the kidney.

rich supply of blood vessels. Some of these blood vessels are tiny capillaries that form structures called *glomeruli* (GLO-MEER-yew-lye). A glomerulus is a tiny, fluffy tangle of capillaries that looks a little like a ball of cotton wool. It is surrounded by a round case called a *Bowman's capsule*. This capsule leads into a narrow tube that twists and turns and finally feeds into a slightly thicker tube called a *collecting tubule*. The Bowman's capsule and the tiny coiled tube that leads from it is called a *nephron* (NEF-ron). It is the working unit of the kidney. A nephron is about half an inch long, but this tube is so thin that you could not see it without a microscope. There are about a million nephrons in each kidney.

The urine formed in the kidneys is gathered in the collecting tubules and finally flows through the ureters into the bladder.

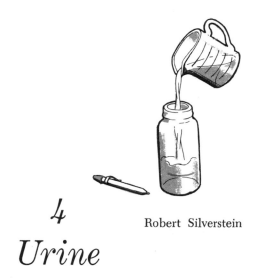

4

Robert Silverstein

Urine

When the subject of urine comes up, people usually become embarrassed. But in many parts of the world urine has been considered a useful substance. The ancients used it as a soap for washing. Some American Indians used urine as a mouthwash. Some South American natives have even used it as a refreshing drink!

You can learn some things about urine through a series of experiments. Get some large jars with lids. Mark off the ounces with a colored marking pen or pencil, by pouring water into the jars from a measuring cup. The next time you urinate, do so into one of the jars. Write down the amount of urine you voided.

Tomorrow when you get up, you can start keeping a daily record of your urination. Write down the time of each urination and the amount of urine voided. Is it the same each time? Do you void more urine if a longer time has passed between urinations?

Keep a record of the amount of water, milk, and other fluids that you drink during the day. Compare it to the amount of urine you void during the day.

After you have kept records for two or three days, you will have a good idea of your normal patterns of urination. Now try adding a *little* extra salt to your foods. (BE CAREFUL! Too much salt is not good for you.) How does this affect your urination?

The next day, go back to your normal diet. Is your urination back to normal? On the following day you can try a new variation. Drink a lot of extra water all day long. How much did you urinate that day? You will probably find that you urinated more than usual.

Another experiment you can try is to hold your urine as long as possible. The first urge will usually pass, and you will find that you may be able to get through another urge or two before you absolutely must urinate. Did you void more urine than usual? Is it as large an amount as you usually would have voided during that period of time?

The amazing story of how urine is formed in the kidneys will help you to understand the results of your experiments. The process really starts in the

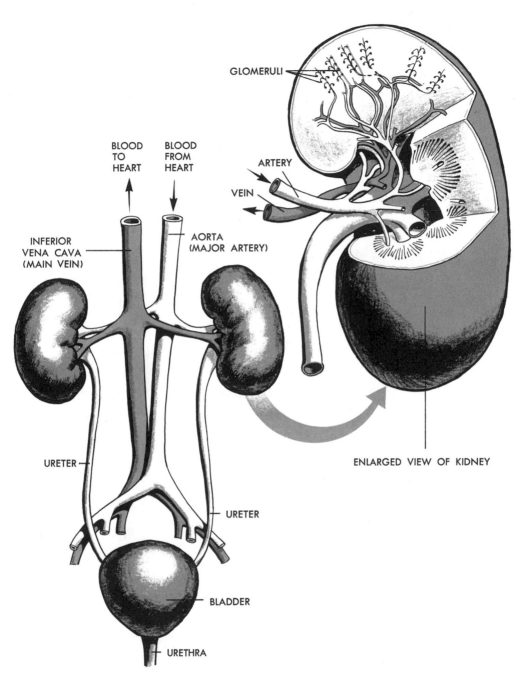

GLOMERULI

ARTERY

VEIN

BLOOD
TO
HEART

BLOOD
FROM
HEART

INFERIOR
VENA CAVA
(MAIN VEIN)

AORTA
(MAJOR ARTERY)

URETER

URETER

ENLARGED VIEW OF KIDNEY

BLADDER

URETHRA

The kidneys work closely with the circulatory system.

bloodstream. Waste products from the cells pass out through their thin outer membranes and then through the walls of tiny blood vessels called capillaries that pass nearby. The waste materials are carried along in the blood flowing in the blood vessels of the body. The blood that flows past the cells of the body travels in capillaries and veins to the heart. This strong pump sends the blood in arteries to the lungs, through the tiny capillaries in the air sacs of the lungs, and back again through veins to the heart. Now the blood is pumped again, out a big artery called the *aorta* (AY-OR-TUH), and down smaller and smaller branching arteries and capillaries to various parts of the body. Some of the blood vessel pathways lead into the tiny glomeruli of the kidneys.

Each minute, more than a quart of blood is pumped through the kidneys—about a quarter of all the blood that is pumped through the heart. In a whole day, about 180 quarts of blood are pumped through the kidneys—about eighteen buckets full!

The work of the kidneys begins in the Bowman's capsule. Water and small chemicals leak out from the blood in the glomerulus through its thin walls, but large molecules, such as proteins, are too big to get through. So the blood that flows on in the capillary is thicker, and a thin, watery fluid collects in the coiled tube of the nephron.

Scientists say that at this stage the kidney works like a filter. A filter is a device that screens out certain things but lets others through. The filter in an air conditioner screens out dust particles but lets air circulate through the room. The oil filter in a car screens out sludge from the oil. The filter on a filter-tip cigarette screens out tars from the cigarette smoke. The liquid that seeps out from the glomerulus is called the *nephric* (NEF-RIK) *filtrate*.

If all your kidneys could do was to filter liquids

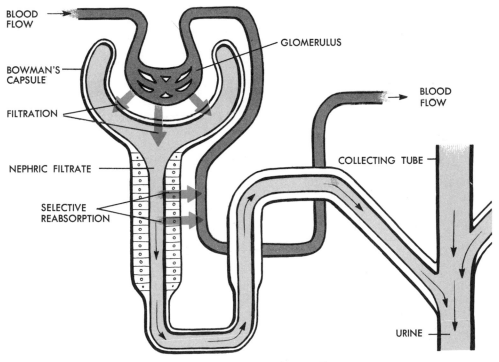

How urine is formed.

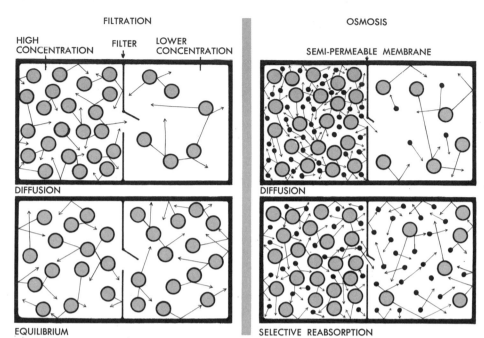

FILTRATION

HIGH CONCENTRATION   FILTER   LOWER CONCENTRATION

OSMOSIS

SEMI-PERMEABLE MEMBRANE

DIFFUSION

DIFFUSION

EQUILIBRIUM

SELECTIVE REABSORPTION

Diffusion plays an important part in the work of the kidneys. Particles tend to move from a region of high concentration to a region of low concentration until an equilibrium is established. If the openings in the partition are too small for some of the particles to pass through, there is a special case of diffusion called *osmosis*.

through the walls of the glomeruli, you would be in serious trouble. You would be losing hundreds of pounds of water every single day! Imagine how much water you would have to drink to make up for that. (A quart of water weighs a little over two pounds.)

The next step of the kidneys' work is called *selective reabsorption*. Water and other substances are reabsorbed or transferred back into the network of capillaries that surround the tiny kidney tubules. This occurs in several ways. Mineral substances, such as sodium and chloride *ions* (EYE-AHNZ) (the ingredients of table salt), potassium, calcium, and carbonate ions (limestone is made of calcium carbonate), are carried through the capillary walls with the help of enzymes. Now the nephric filtrate is very thin and watery, while inside the capillaries there is a high concentration of proteins, salts, and other chemicals, and a very low concentration of water.

Molecules and ions, the tiny units that make up the chemicals of the body, are constantly in motion. Usually they do not get very far, for they quickly bump into other molecules or ions and bounce back. But scientists have found that something unusual happens when the concentration of one type of molecule is greater in one region than in the region next to it. After awhile, more molecules move into the region of lower concentration than move out of it. Eventually the two concentrations are the same. This process is called *diffusion* (DIF-FEW-zHUN).

For example, picture two rooms next to each other, connected by an open door. In one room, several dozen balloons are bouncing around. Soon some of the balloons will bounce into the other room. Since there are still fewer balloons in the other room, new balloons will bounce in more often than the balloons already there will bounce out. After a time, there will be about the same number of balloons in each room. The number of balloons bouncing through the door in one direction will now be about the same as the number going in the opposite direction. An *equilibrium* (EE-QWIH-LIB-REE-UM) has been reached.

But what if the doorway that connects the two rooms is a very small doorway? And suppose one room contains small balloons that can fit easily through the doorway, while the other room is filled with balloons that are too big to go through at all. After a while, the little balloons will diffuse into the other room, so that the concentrations of these balloons in the two rooms are about the same. But the big balloons cannot diffuse into the other room because they cannot fit through the doorway. So there will still be a large difference in the concentrations of big balloons, even after an equilibrium has been reached for the small ones.

This is a special case of diffusion, when it occurs through a barrier that will permit some particles to pass, but not others. This kind of barrier is called a *semipermeable* (SEM-EE-PER-MEE-A-BUL) *membrane*, and diffusion through it is called *osmosis* (OZ-MOHS-IS).

The walls of the capillaries are semipermeable membranes. (Remember that only small molecules such as water and salts filtered through the glomeruli, and larger protein molecules could not?) Osmosis accounts for another important part of selective reabsorption. At first there is a much higher concentration of water in the kidney tubules than there is in the capillaries next to them. The tiny water molecules easily diffuse through the semipermeable membranes and flow into the capillaries. But the larger molecules held in the capillaries are kept there and cannot diffuse out.

The name "selective reabsorption" may suggest to you that a choice is being made about which chemicals are being reabsorbed in the kidneys. This is quite true. If the amount of a particular substance in the blood in the capillaries is unusually low, a large amount of it will be reabsorbed from the kidney tubules. In this way, the kidneys help the body to avoid getting rid of substances that it really needs. If the concentration of some substance in the blood is unusually high, very little of it will be reabsorbed. The body can thus get rid of the excess in the urine. In the disease *diabetes mellitus* (DYE-A-BEET-EEZ MEL-LYTE-US), for example, there is an unusually high concentration of sugar in the blood. As a result, very little sugar is reabsorbed in the kidneys, and sugar passes out of the body in the urine. This does not happen normally, and so a test for diabetes is for the presence of sugar in the urine. In fact, this condition gave the disease its name. "Mellitus" means "sweet"; some brave doctor discovered the symptom by tasting his patient's urine.

Many diseases and other conditions can be discovered by tests of the urine. For example, during pregnancy, large amounts of a female sex hormone are secreted. This chemical is small enough to pass into the kidney tubules during filtration in the glomeruli. It is normally selectively reabsorbed. But if the woman is pregnant, the concentration of the sex hormone in her blood is so high that some of this hormone remains in the urine. There are various laboratory tests for this chemical. And so a woman who wishes to know if she is pregnant can bring a sample of her urine to a laboratory for testing.

Selective reabsorption is the reason why you do not have to drink a hundred quarts of water each day. Most of the water that passes through the kidneys is reabsorbed, and only a quart or so a day is actually excreted. The amount of water that is reabsorbed depends on a number of things. If you drink more water than usual, more fluid will be excreted in your urine. For the kidneys help the body to maintain its delicate balance, keeping conditions inside the body as constant as possible. This delicate, carefully maintained equilibrium of the body conditions is called *homeostasis* (HOME-EE-OH-STAY-SIS).

If you drink less fluid than usual, your urine will be more concentrated. In fact, it may become so concentrated that it will irritate the delicate membrane lining the urethra. Then you may feel a burning sensation when you urinate. Very hot weather, which makes you sweat a lot, may also cause urine to be more concentrated. In each case, the kidneys reabsorb more water than usual, so that it is conserved for the body.

But under some conditions, even the kidneys cannot maintain homeostasis. For example, a person lost in the desert, under the burning sun, will lose a great deal of water in sweat. He will not lose as much water as usual in his urine, but he still will lose some. (For there must be some water to flush out the nitrogen compounds and other solid wastes.) If he has no water to drink, his body will become *dehydrated* (DEE-HYE-DRAYT-ED) or dried out. Some people have managed to save themselves under such conditions by drinking their own urine. In that way they saved the precious fluids and salts that their bodies would have otherwise lost.

In your experiments, did you find that you urinated less when you ate a lot of salty foods? This may have occurred even if you drank extra water because the salt made you feel thirsty. Extra salt in the tissues causes extra water to be kept in the body. The extra water is needed to keep the salt concentrations in the blood and tissues constantly at just the right levels for the body reactions to take place. Eventually, if the kidneys are healthy, they will get rid of the extra salt and then eliminate the extra water from the tissues, too.

Pregnant women, people with heart disease, and people who spend a lot of time on their feet sometimes have trouble with extra fluids in their legs. Their ankles and feet may become swollen and painful. In order to get rid of this excess fluid, the body must get rid of salt, because salt and water maintain an osmotic balance in the body. Doctors suggest two ways to get rid of salt in the body: by reducing the intake of salt (which most people find very difficult) and by taking a drug called a *diuretic* (DYE-YURE-ET-IK) which helps the kidneys to get rid of the excess water by increasing the elimination of salts.

Sometimes calcium salts in the urine separate to form crystals in the kidneys. These crystals may be like tiny grains of sand. Or they may grow so large that they nearly fill the kidney passages. Small particles of *kidney sand* may pass out of the body through the *urethra* when the person urinates. He may never realize they were there at all. But larger *kidney stones* may become extremely painful as they press on the tissues and block the flow of urine. Large kidney stones may have to be removed by an operation. Then the doctor will probably advise his patient to drink unusually large amounts of water so that his urine will be too dilute for new kidney stones to form.

For some reason which scientists do not entirely understand, the kidneys are able to increase their selective reabsorption during the night, when you are sleeping. You have probably noticed that you can go much longer between urinations at night than you can during the day, when you are active. (This is partly due to the fact that you are not taking in any liquids while you are sleeping.) The first urine that you void in the morning contains less water than unsual, and so it is darker and stronger smelling than the urine of the rest of the day. This daily pattern of changes in selective reabsorption is not something that you are born with. A young baby wets its diaper regularly throughout the day and night. But after a year or two or three, about the same time the child learns to control the sphincter muscles that close his bladder, his kidneys develop the ability to reabsorb extra water during the night.

A failure to reabsorb extra water at night may wake you up and send you to the bathroom. Or, if you do not wake up, you may wet the bed. Bed-wetting is a problem for many children long past the age when they are supposed to have been toilet trained. There are many theories about what causes bed-wetting and what to do about it. Some

Scientists are studying the causes and cures of bedwetting.

doctors believe that it occurs when the bladder is not large enough, and they recommend a series of exercises to increase the capacity of the bladder. Some recommend a buzzer arrangement that rings as soon as the bedclothes are wet and wakes the child up. Other doctors are convinced that bed-wetting is caused by emotional problems and should be treated by discovering and relieving the problems. In laboratories where researchers study patterns of sleep, it has been discovered that bed-wetting starts in the deepest stage of sleep, when people do not usually dream. Some researchers believe that a child who wets the bed has a nervous system that is a little slower to mature than the average. (This does not mean that he is any less intelligent than the average child.)

The main nitrogen compound in the urine is a substance called *urea* (YEW-REE-UH). Urea is not made in the kidneys. It is produced in the liver. Waste ammonia and carbon dioxide are carried away from the body cells in the blood that flows past them. The blood flows eventually to the liver, where ammonia is combined with carbon dioxide to form urea. Urea is carried by the blood out of the liver to the kidneys, where it seeps out of the glomeruli and so passes into the nephric filtrate. (Urea is a small molecule.) Urea is much less poisonous than ammonia, but too much of it is still not very healthy for the body. During selective reabsorption, urea stays in the kidney tubules. After this process is finished, there is more than sixty times as much urea in the urine as there was in the original nephric filtrate.

If urine is allowed to stand around in contact with air, some of the urea breaks down into ammonia and carbon dioxide. That is why old urine has a much stronger smell than fresh urine. It was the high ammonia content that made urine such a useful "cleaning fluid" for the ancients.

In addition to filtration in the Bowman's capsules and selective reabsorption, there is another process that plays a role in excretion through the kidneys. It is called *tubular secretion.* Cells of the kidney tubules actively remove substances from the blood in the nearby capillaries and secrete them into the channel that leads to the ureters. Tubular secretion plays an important role in removing certain dyes and drugs from the blood. For example, if you are ill and the doctor prescribes penicillin, traces of the drug will soon appear in your urine. Urine tests can also reveal whether a person is taking drugs such as heroin.

Even though you may need to go to the bathroom only a few times a day, urine is forming all the time in your kidneys. It trickles drop by drop through the collecting tubules, along the ureters, and into the bladder. Gradually the bladder swells up like a balloon. When it is full, special nerve endings in the bladder wall send messages to the brain. Now you get a feeling of fullness in your lower abdomen and an urge to urinate. When you are ready to urinate, messages are sent to a control center in your spinal cord, which in turn sends messages to the bladder. The sphincter muscles relax and the bladder walls contract. The urine is then forced out of the bladder, through the urethra, and out of the body. In a young baby, this is all done automatically, without his thinking about it. But gradually the baby learns to control his bladder muscles and to urinate only when he wants to.

5

Other Means of Excretion

Do you have smelly feet? Most of us do. There are many sweat glands in the skin of the feet. In most other parts of the body, sweat can evaporate into the air so easily that we often do not even have a feeling of being wet. But feet are usually wrapped up tightly in shoes and socks. The skin of the feet stays moist and provides an excellent environment for bacteria. It is these skin bacteria that make feet smell. They feed on bits of dead skin and on the moisture and nutrients provided by the sweat itself. If you wash your feet carefully each day and use a powder to help keep them dry, you can keep your smelly skin bacteria from multiplying too quickly.

There are more than two million sweat glands in your skin, and some parts of the body have more than others. The palms of the hands, the soles of the feet, the underarms, the scalp, and the forehead are especially richly supplied with sweat

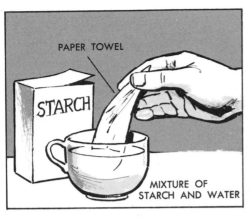

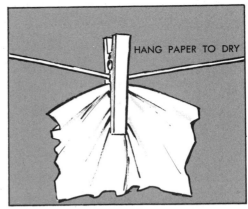

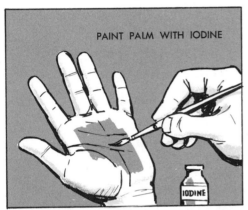

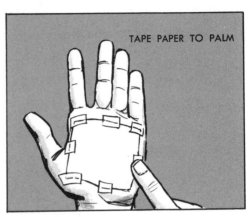

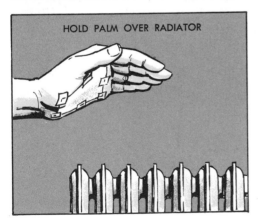

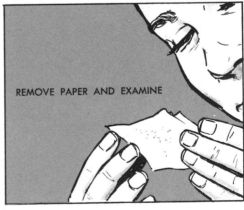

Mapping the sweat glands.

glands. Have you ever seen someone break out with beads of moisture on his forehead and upper lip, when it was very hot or when he was working very hard?

Each sweat gland is a tiny coiled tube that starts deep in the skin and empties out at the surface, through a tiny pinpoint opening called a pore. You can make a map of the sweat pores in the palm of your hand. Mix a teaspoonful of instant starch with a cupful of water, and then dip a piece of filter paper or paper towel into it. Hang the paper

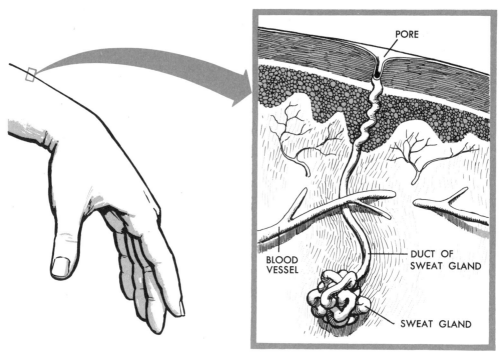

Sweat glands in the skin function as excretory organs.

up to dry. When it is ready, paint the palm of your hand with tincture of iodine and let it dry. Now press the dry starch paper against the skin of your palm and tape it on securely.

Tincture of iodine is a solution of iodine in alcohol, and it has a brown color. But iodine can react with starch to form a compound with a dark blue color. This reaction takes place only when there is moisture about. There is no moisture on your dry palm or on the dry starch paper. Now place your hand over a warm radiator or jump up and down so that you will sweat. A tiny drop of moisture will form in each sweat pore. At those spots, the iodine will react with the starch, and a little blue dot will form on the starch paper. When you take the paper off your palm, you will have a map of all the sweat glands in your palm. Now try the same experiment on another part of your body—the skin of your forearm, for example—and see whether the dots are farther apart.

The sweat glands are part of the excretory system. These glands get rid of excess water, of course. But the watery sweat also contains dissolved salts, urea, and various other chemicals. In fact, sweat is really like a very dilute urine. The sweat glands also help to rid the body of excess heat. Heat is a major by-product of many of the chemical reactions in the body. If this heat were allowed to build up, it would heat up all the body cells. It might make them so hot that enzymes and other delicate body chemicals would be destroyed. It would be like being cooked alive.

Heat is radiating out of your body through your skin all the time. But if it is very hot outside, this means of cooling the skin does not work very well. Fortunately the sweat glands provide an even more effective way of getting rid of excess body heat. You know that you sweat much more when it is hot outside.

The sweat glands are effective cooling systems for the body because of some special properties of water. First of all, water can hold an unusually large amount of heat. The water of the blood carries heat away from the body cells. Blood flows through tiny capillaries that pass near the sweat glands. Water diffuses out through the capillary walls, through the tissues of the skin, and into the tiny tubules of the sweat glands. More heat is radiated out and heats up the water in the sweat glands. The water turns into a vapor, and much of the sweat that the sweat glands excrete actually passes out of the body in the form of a gas. The sweat carries out all its stored-up heat and so helps to cool the body.

Hard work and physical exercise can also make you sweat more than usual. For muscle cells make a great deal of heat when they work. An average

Emotional tension and physical exercise can cause an increase in sweating.

adult sweats about a quart of liquid each day. But if he is working hard and the temperature is very high, he may lose as much as three quarts of water in a day! Emotions, too, can make a person sweat more than usual. Have you ever felt sweat trickling down your back and in your armpits just before a big test? With all these things working together —heat, nervousness, and muscular exercise—a major league baseball pitcher often loses ten pounds or more during a single close game.

Too much sweating can be dangerous. The body cannot spare all that water. And salts and other chemicals are lost along with the water. The kidneys can adjust their selective reabsorption to make up for some of the loss. But even they need to use some water. That is why you have to drink extra water or other liquids during hot summer weather. You should also take some extra salt, to make up for what you lose by sweating.

The sweat glands and the kidneys work together to take care of two of the body's most important waste products, water and nitrogen compounds. They also get rid of some carbon dioxide, combined with ammonia in the compound urea. But most of the waste carbon dioxide is removed from the body in another way: through the lungs.

The blood flowing through the tiny capillaries that pass by nearly every living cell of the body, brings the cells fresh oxygen and food materials. The waste products diffuse out of the cells through the cell membranes and into the capillaries through the capillary walls.

The blood flows back through veins to the heart, and then it is sent to the lungs. The tiny capillaries that criss-cross through the lungs have extremely thin walls. Gases can easily pass back and forth through the capillary walls. They pass just as easily in and out of the *alveoli* (AL-VEE-OH-LYE) or tiny air sacs of the lungs.

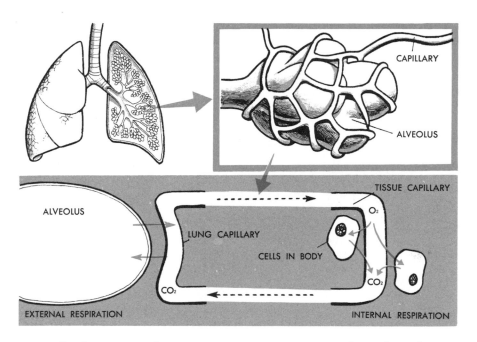

CAPILLARY

ALVEOLUS

TISSUE CAPILLARY

ALVEOLUS

LUNG CAPILLARY

CELLS IN BODY

O_2

CO_2

CO_2

EXTERNAL RESPIRATION

INTERNAL RESPIRATION

The lungs are the main organ excreting carbon dioxide. The gas exchange takes place in tiny air sacs called *alveoli.*

The air that you breathe in contains about twenty-one percent oxygen and only four-hundredths percent carbon dioxide. The air that you breathe out contains only sixteen percent oxygen and four percent carbon dioxide. What happened?

The blood flowing into the lungs has a very low concentration of oxygen and a very high concentration of carbon dioxide. The air that you breathe into your lungs has a high concentration of oxygen and a low concentration of carbon dioxide. So oxygen diffuses out of the alveoli and into the capillaries. Carbon dioxide diffuses out of the capillaries

41

and into the alveoli. As a result of this gas exchange, the blood has a fresh supply of oxygen to carry to the body cells, and the waste carbon dioxide is breathed out of the lungs into the air.

Your lungs also excrete water vapor. (You can see a mist of water droplets when you breathe out on a frosty day.) And they get rid of some excess heat. Did you ever see a dog panting on a hot day? A dog gets rid of excess heat by the evaporation of water from its mouth.

The other main highway for getting rid of the body's wastes is the intestines. The food you eat is *digested,* or broken down into smaller chemicals that your body can use, in various organs of the digestive system. The mouth, the stomach, and various glands that empty into the small intestine all contribute enzymes and other digestive chemicals that help to break down food. A few food substances are absorbed into the bloodstream through the walls of the stomach. But most absorption occurs in the small intestine.

Not everything you eat can be used by the body for food. Vegetables, for example, contain plant fibers that your digestive system cannot break down. These solid waste materials are pushed along through the intestines by rhythmic contractions of the intestinal walls. In the large intestines, excess water is absorbed, and the undigested food

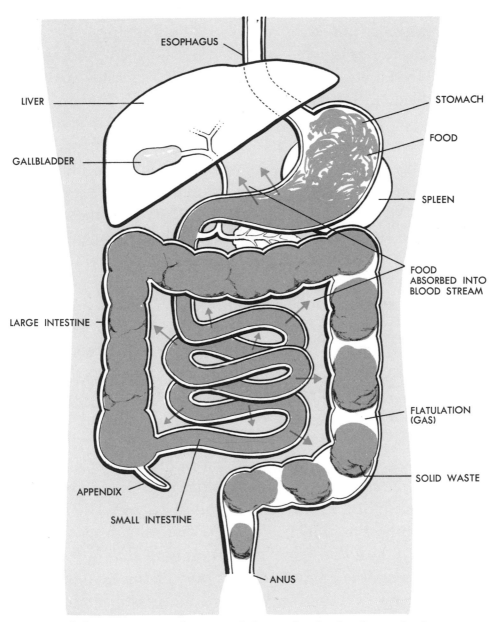

ESOPHAGUS

LIVER

GALLBLADDER

STOMACH

FOOD

SPLEEN

FOOD ABSORBED INTO BLOOD STREAM

LARGE INTESTINE

FLATULATION (GAS)

SOLID WASTE

APPENDIX

SMALL INTESTINE

ANUS

Solid wastes are eliminated from the body through the large intestine.

materials, joined by masses of multiplying bacteria, are gradually molded into solid feces.

In the intestines, various other body wastes are added to the undigested food materials. For example, red blood cells become very fragile when they get old. (A red cell lives about 120 days.) In the spleen, the red cells must squeeze in and out of tiny holes in the blood capillaries. This is very hard on an old red cell, and its thin membrane breaks, spilling out the red pigment *hemoglobin* (HEE-MOH-GLOH-BIN). The hemoglobin is captured by spleen cells and other cells in the body that serve as roving trouble-shooters. These cells change hemoglobin into a substance called *bilirubin* (BILL-EE-ROO-BIN). The bilirubin is combined with the blood proteins and carried to the liver. The liver frees bilirubin from the blood proteins and sends some of it through the blood to the kidneys, where it passes out of the body. The rest of the bilirubin is excreted from the liver out into the intestines in the mixture called *bile*. (The word "bilirubin" actually means "bile red.") It is the bilirubin, which is changed into a substance called *urobilin* (YEW-ROH-BILL-IN), that gives the feces their brown color. Some of this colored substance is also absorbed in the intestines and makes its way through the blood into the urine. Urine, of course, is much less concentrated than feces. That is why it is yellow instead of brown.

If the liver is not working properly (or the *gall-bladder,* in which bile is stored, is blocked), bile pigments can build up in the bloodstream. This can also happen in blood diseases in which red blood cells are broken down too fast for the liver to keep up with them. A condition called *jaundice* (JAWN-DIS) results. The person's skin turns yellow because the bile pigments in the skin capillaries show through. Even the whites of his eyes turn yellow. A knowledge of how bilirubin is formed, and how it is excreted by the kidneys, helps doctors to determine just where the trouble lies and how serious it is.

6
Excretion in Water Animals

After a rainstorm, puddles shimmer in ditches along the side of the road. The rainwater that fell from the sky was pure (except for some particulates and assorted other pollutants that were washed down on the way). But within hours, the puddle is swarming with life. Tiny cysts of microscopic water creatures are blown through the air, land in the puddle, and miraculously come to life. Algae spread a scum of green threads across the puddle as they use energy from the sun to grow and multiply. Euglenas and their relatives dart jerkily to and fro, propelled by their lashing, whip-like *flagella* (FLA-JELL-UH). Paramecia swim gracefully with their tiny waving *cilia* (SILL-EE-UH). Blob-like amebas ooze along the bottom, stretching out their jelly-like bodies to engulf their prey.

Life in the puddle can be difficult for the tiny creatures. Not only are there other lurking creatures that might eat them, but even the water itself can be an enemy. The water in the puddle is nearly pure water. But the fluid inside the body of a paramecium or ameba or euglena has a high concentration of salts and other dissolved chemicals. Water diffuses in through the thin membrane that surrounds the one-celled creature's body. If there were no way to get the extra water out, the poor creature would burst.

The ameba, the euglena, the paramecium, and other one-celled creatures of ponds and puddles solve their water problem with a structure called a *contractile vacuole* (VAK-YEW-OLE). The extra water is sent into a small cavity inside the body. When the vacuole is filled with water, it contracts violently and pumps the water out of the cell. The ameba does not seem to keep its contractile vac-

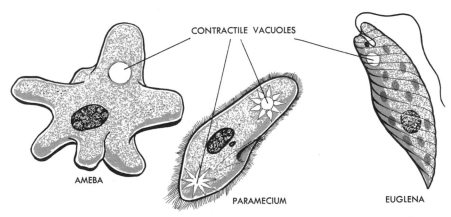

CONTRACTILE VACUOLES

AMEBA

PARAMECIUM

EUGLENA

Single-celled pond organisms generally have contractile vacuoles to get rid of excess water. Most other wastes pass out of the body by diffusion through the cell membrane.

uole in any one particular place. (How could it, when it is constantly changing its body shape?) But the paramecium, which has a firmer shape, has two contractile vacuoles that remain in specific parts of its body. (One is above the paramecium's mouth, and the other is below it.) When the water is pumped out, it always comes out the same pores in the paramecium's outer covering.

Water is the only real excretory problem that one-celled pond creatures have. Ammonia, carbon dioxide, and other waste materials can easily diffuse out through the cell membrane and be carried away in the water of the pond or puddle.

Some of the simpler animals that live in the sea have even fewer excretory problems. The water concentration in sea water and the water concentration inside a sponge's body, for example, are just about the same. So the sponge can take care of all of its excretion by simple diffusion through the membranes of its cells.

For a more highly organized animal like a flatworm, the problem becomes more complicated. Many cells of a flatworm's body are in inside layers that are not in contact with the water of the pond in which it lives. Simple diffusion cannot help these cells. The flatworm needs an organized excretory system to cope with its wastes. Special cells

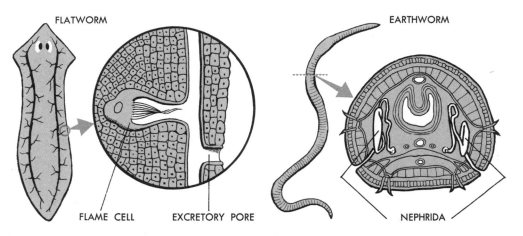

FLATWORM

EARTHWORM

FLAME CELL   EXCRETORY PORE

NEPHRIDA

Higher organisms need more complicated excretory organs. The flatworm has flame cells and the earthworm excretes through nephridia.

called *flame cells* take nitrogen compounds and other wastes from the body fluids and send them down excretory tubules. A fringe of cilia on each flame cell waves back and forth and helps to send the fluid along. These cilia make the flame cell look like a flickering candle flame, and that is where it got its name.

An earthworm is a land animal, but its body is constantly surrounded by a film of water in the soil. Each segment of the earthworm's body has a pair of structures called *nephridia* (NEF-RID-EE-UH), which work very much like nephrons. The nephridium is a tubule, surrounded by a coil of capillaries. Waste materials diffuse out of the capillaries and into the nephridia, where they are concentrated and finally sent out of the body.

Fish have kidneys very much like ours, but they have very different excretory problems, which depend on whether they live in fresh water or in salt water.

Fresh-water fish face the same problem as amebas and paramecia: the water in which they live has a higher water concentration than the fluid inside their bodies. Water cannot diffuse in through the fishes' scales, but it passes in easily through the delicate gill membranes through which the fish breathe. All this water provides one advantage. The fish do not have to bother changing their waste ammonia to urea. They flush out the ammonia mainly by simple diffusion through their gills. There is so much water that the ammonia never gets concentrated enough to do their tissues any harm. But all this extra water has to be pumped out. The force for the pump is provided by the contractions of the heart, which sends the blood through the capillaries, out through the glomeruli, and into the Bowman's capsule. The salts that are lost along with the water are reclaimed by selective reabsorption in the capillaries surrounding the kidney tubules. In fresh-water fish,

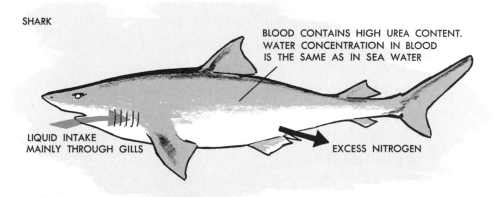

SHARK

BLOOD CONTAINS HIGH UREA CONTENT.
WATER CONCENTRATION IN BLOOD
IS THE SAME AS IN SEA WATER

LIQUID INTAKE
MAINLY THROUGH GILLS

EXCESS NITROGEN

SALT-WATER FISH

STEADY WATER LOSS BY OSMOSIS

CONTINUOUSLY
DRINKS WATER

SALTS EXCRETED BY GILLS   LITTLE URINE

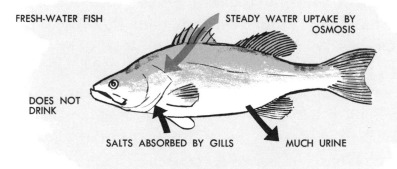

FRESH-WATER FISH

STEADY WATER UPTAKE BY
OSMOSIS

DOES NOT
DRINK

SALTS ABSORBED BY GILLS   MUCH URINE

Salt-water fish have different excretory problems from
fresh-water fish and cope with them differently.

the kidneys are more a means of getting rid of water than of excreting nitrogen wastes.

The problems that salt-water fish face are quite different. The water they live in has a quite high salt concentration. Water would normally tend to be lost out of the fish's body rather than diffusing into it. Salt-water fishes have found two ways to solve this problem.

Sharks and their relatives have very unusual blood. Human blood contains only about a hundredth of a percent of urea. Much more would be poisonous. But sharks' blood contains about two-and-a-half percent urea—more than a hundred times as much. Somehow sharks and their relatives have gained an ability to survive without being harmed by all this urea in their blood. With it, the water concentration in their blood is about the same as that of the oceans they live in. They do not have any water problems, and they use their kidneys to get rid of extra nitrogen compounds, just as humans do. (But a shark's kidney tubules reabsorb much more urea than yours do.)

The bony fishes of the sea, such as tuna, cod, and swordfish, have found a different solution. Their blood has a higher water concentration than sea water, and so they lose water constantly. They replace the water by drinking sea water. Their bodies are able to take the salt out of sea water and get rid of it through the gills. Very little water passes through the kidneys of these fish. In fact, some salt-water fish have no glomeruli at all. They get rid of their nitrogen wastes by tubular secretion.

Sea turtles solve their water and salt problems in much the same way as the bony fishes. So do gulls and other sea birds, which often spend long periods away from fresh water. They drink sea water, and take out the salt in two salt glands in the upper part of the head. The extra salt is sent from the salt glands out of the body in a very concentrated solution through the bird's nostrils.

7

Excretion in Land Animals

A frog lives in two worlds. He spends part of his time swimming in the water, and part of the time hopping about on dry land. He has a thin skin, through which water and gases pass easily. In the pond, the frog's main problem is to get rid of the extra water that diffuses in through his skin. Here his kidneys work mainly as pumps to get rid of this water. But on land, the frog is in danger of drying out. If he does, he will die. Although he has a pair of lungs, he gets part of the oxygen he needs by an exchange of gases through his moist skin. The frog on land can adjust to his new problem in several ways. He can cut down the amount of water filtering through the glomeruli. And he can reabsorb water from his bladder back into his blood, making up for the water he loses by evaporation through his skin.

Saving water is an important problem for all

land animals. Without an easy source of replacement from the outside environment, any water that is lost must be replaced by drinking and eating. Mammals save some water by excreting urea instead of ammonia. Because urea is less poisonous, it does not have to be diluted with as much water to keep it from harming the body cells. But birds and desert reptiles go one step further. They can change their nitrogen wastes into another substance, *uric* (YURE-ik) *acid*. This chemical does not dissolve in water, so it can be excreted with practically no water at all.

Some lizards and snakes have no glomeruli at all. Others have small glomeruli. They filter out just enough water to wash their uric acid wastes into a chamber called the *cloaca* (KLOII-AY-KUH). Reptiles' urine, feces, and sex cells all pass through the cloaca on their way out of the body. (The name "cloaca" comes from a Latin word meaning "sewer.") In the cloaca, the small amount of water in the urine is reabsorbed. From time to time, the reptile empties its cloaca of the brownish feces and pasty white uric acid that have accumulated.

With these efficient means of saving water, a desert reptile can survive without drinking any water at all. It gets all the water it needs from the food it eats and the chemical reactions in its body.

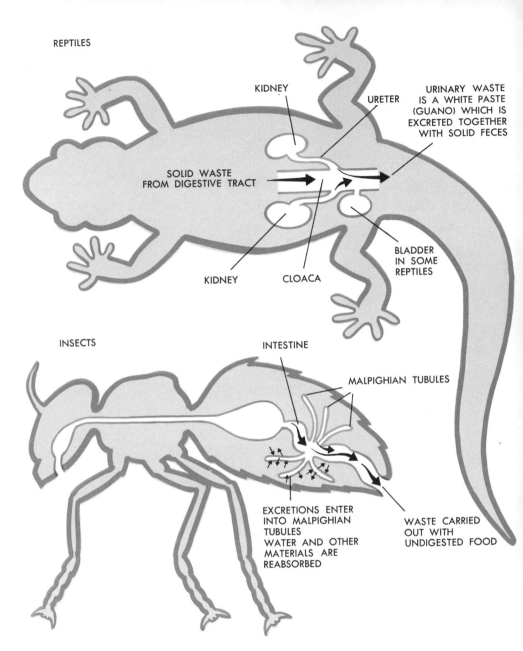

REPTILES

KIDNEY

URETER

URINARY WASTE
IS A WHITE PASTE
(GUANO) WHICH IS
EXCRETED TOGETHER
WITH SOLID FECES

SOLID WASTE
FROM DIGESTIVE TRACT

BLADDER
IN SOME
REPTILES

KIDNEY

CLOACA

INSECTS

INTESTINE

MALPIGHIAN TUBULES

EXCRETIONS ENTER
INTO MALPIGHIAN
TUBULES
WATER AND OTHER
MATERIALS ARE
REABSORBED

WASTE CARRIED
OUT WITH
UNDIGESTED FOOD

Both birds and reptiles excrete urine and feces through
a single opening from a common chamber, the cloaca.
Their nitrogen wastes are in the form of uric acid, which
does not have to be diluted with water. Insects collect
wastes for excretion with organs called malpighian tubules.

Birds have solved the problem of saving water in much the same way as lizards and snakes. They excrete nitrogen wastes in the form of uric acid. (That is the whitish stuff that pigeons leave on statues and city streets.) Birds can absorb water in their kidney tubules so effectively that their urine is quite concentrated.

A few mammals, too, have adapted unusually well to life in dry places. The kangaroo rat, which lives in the desert regions of the western United States, excretes a urine more than four times as concentrated as human urine. This little rodent also saves water by staying in its burrow during the hottest times of the day. Shut inside, in the damp air of its burrow, it does not lose much water by evaporation. The kangaroo rat conserves water so well that it never has to drink any liquid at all, even though it lives on dry seeds. It gets the water it needs from chemical reactions in its body.

Amphibians, reptiles, birds, and mammals are all close relatives of ours, and they all have kidneys that help in excretion. Another widespread group of animals, the insects, has taken different paths of development and found different answers to the problems of life.

Insects do have excretory systems, but these consist of organs called *malpighian* (MAL-PIG-EE-AN) *tubules.* Waste products diffuse from the insect's body cavity into these tubes and are emptied into the digestive system. They are carried out with the undigested food.

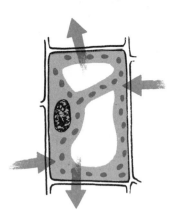

8

Excretion in Plants

Compared to animals, plants have very few waste products. But even these small amounts must be gotten rid of, or else the plant will wither and die.

Most of the plant's waste products pass out as gases through tiny holes in the plant leaves. These holes are called *stomates* (STOH-MATES). Each one is guarded by two kidney-bean-shaped cells called *guard cells.* The guard cells can expand to close the stomates and contract to open them. Plants save some water by almost completely closing the stomates at night. But during the day they must keep these holes open, for the carbon dioxide that they need as a raw material from which to make their food, comes in through the stomates with the air. Through the open holes, plants lose an enormous amount of water. An average corn plant loses about fifty gallons of water through its

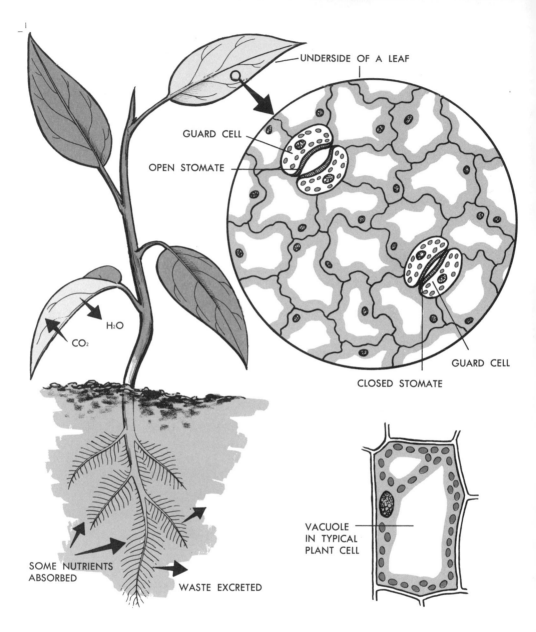

UNDERSIDE OF A LEAF

GUARD CELL

OPEN STOMATE

GUARD CELL

CLOSED STOMATE

H_2O

CO_2

SOME NUTRIENTS ABSORBED

WASTE EXCRETED

VACUOLE IN TYPICAL PLANT CELL

Plants generally have less complicated excretory problems than animals and do not need a special excretory system.

leaves during the growing season, and a medium-sized tree will lose that much water in a single day. Water must be taken in constantly through the plant's roots to replace what is lost.

Some waste materials diffuse out into the soil through the delicate covering of the roots. It has been found that some of the chemical waste products, that plants send out into the air and soil, influence other plants around them. They may keep certain plants from growing too close, and they may help the growth of certain other plants.

Plants have a few other ways of getting rid of poisonous wastes. They may seal them off in a little compartment called a *vacuole*. Safely walled up, the waste materials cannot harm the plant tissues. Spinach plants accumulate a waste material called *oxalic acid* in their leaves in the form of solid crystals. When the older leaves wither and drop off, the plant gets rid of the oxalic acid that they contain.

There are a number of reasons why plants can get along with such simple means of excretion, while animals need complicated excretory systems to get rid of their wastes.

First of all, not as many chemical breakdown reactions occur in plants as in animals, and so waste products build up more slowly. One of the major excretory problems in animals is how to get rid of nitrogen wastes, for their bodies are made mainly of proteins, which contain nitrogen. But plants have a much larger amount of carbohydrates, which contain only carbon, hydrogen, and oxygen, and no nitrogen at all. So plants do not have nearly as much nitrogen wastes as animals do. A third reason is that plants seem to be better able than animals to use their waste products and build them into new chemicals before they can accumulate enough to harm the tissues. When ammonia is produced, plants build it into new proteins. Carbon dioxide and water are produced when plants "breathe," just as in animals, but plants can build these substances into new carbohydrates and other food materials.

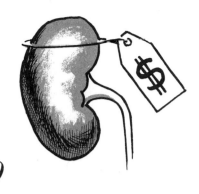

9

Frontiers of Research on Excretion

Recently there was an unusual ad in the paper. A man was offering three thousand dollars to anyone who would donate a kidney to him. This man had a kidney disease: his kidneys could no longer work to clean out the poisons from his blood. For two years he had been receiving treatments with a kidney machine.

The kidney machine is a device that can substitute for a person's own kidneys when they are not working properly. The person's bloodstream is hooked up to tubes that carry the blood over a series of membranes. Poisons from the blood pass through the membranes in a special form of diffusion called *dialysis* (DYE-AL-IH-SIS), and the blood is then returned to the body. Each treatment takes five to twelve hours, and the person must have treatments two to three times a week. The first kidney machines could be used only in hospitals and were very expensive. It cost about twenty thousand dollars a year to keep a single patient alive. Now home units are available that can be run by a member of the patient's family at a cost of several thousand dollars a year. More than three thousand people in the United States are now being kept alive by kidney machines.

But life on a kidney machine is not an easy life. Two or three days a week is a lot of time to lose tied to a machine, and the treatment is a terrible strain on the family member who must help. The patient must be watched carefully at all times. If he dozes off and the tubes pull loose, he can bleed to death. Sometimes there are bad side effects. The person may become depressed. He may suffer from constant pain, or he may itch all over. The man who advertised for a kidney donor had all these symptoms.

Doctors believe that it is far better to have a new kidney transplanted into the body than to receive treatments from a kidney machine. The transplant kidneys can be obtained from the body of a person who has just died. Or a living person can donate one of his two kidneys, for one normal kidney can carry the load alone.

Doctors prefer to use a kidney from a close relative. The tissues of the relative are often very

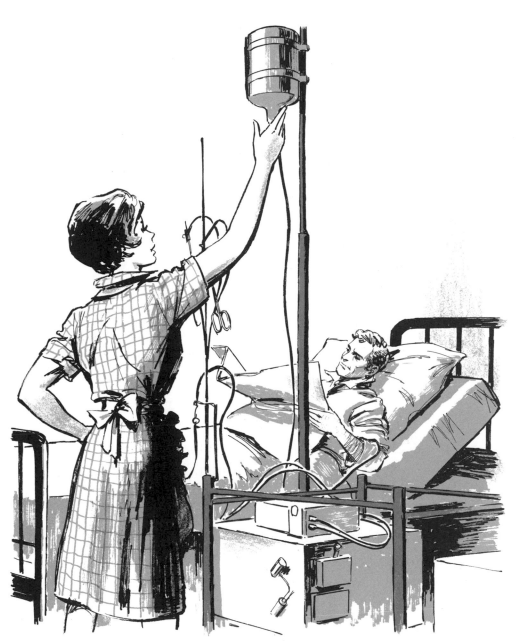

Dialysis machines that can be used at home are now saving the lives of many people with kidney diseases.

similar to those of the patient. In this way, one of the most serious problems of organ transplants may be overcome. For the body has a defense system that can recognize "foreign" substances and attack them. This defense system protects us from diseases. But when an organ is transplanted, the body's defense system may attack the new organ and cause it to shrivel and die. The organ is said to be rejected. If the suffering patient has an identical twin who can donate a kidney, there will be no problem of rejection, for the tissues of identical twins are just about identical. The tissues of relatives are not identical, but they are usually closer to the patient's than a stranger's. Drugs can also be used to keep the body's defense system from attacking a transplanted kidney. But these drugs are dangerous. They prevent the body from attacking *any* foreign invaders, including disease bacteria. Patients taking anti-rejection drugs sometimes die from pneumonia or other infections, even though their new kidney is working perfectly. Anti-rejection drugs also seem to interfere with the body's means of fighting the growth of cancerous tumors. Doctors are now finding that cancer is more likely to appear in transplant patients treated with anti-rejection drugs.

Even with all these difficulties, more than four thousand kidney transplants have been performed, and many people have been given a new chance for life.

Scientists are now working on smaller, cheaper, more efficient kidney machines. They hope to develop an artificial kidney that is compact and long-lasting enough to be placed in the body and left there to function effectively for years. Indeed, a workable "artificial kidney" does not have to look like a kidney or even work exactly like one. A promising approach that has already been successful in tests on animals is the use of tiny granules of specially treated charcoal, coated with a plastic material. A person whose kidneys are not working would swallow a number of these tiny "pills." They would pass through his stomach and intestines, but their plastic coating would keep them from being digested. On their way through the digestive tract, waste products and poisons would pass into the granules and be trapped by the charcoal inside them. The granules would pass out of the body in the feces, carrying with them many of the wastes that the kidneys would normally excrete. Then the patient would swallow a new supply.

Every year, nearly a hundred thousand Americans die from kidney ailments. When these techniques are perfected, many more of these people will be saved.

The artificial kidney is the major frontier of research on the excretory system. Another exciting area of research has grown out of the program of space exploration.

Imagine a long voyage on a spaceship—perhaps to Mars, or even beyond. Astronauts are human beings and, like everyone else, their bodies must get rid of their waste products. They breathe out carbon dioxide and water vapor, and they excrete other wastes in the form of sweat, urine, and feces. What happens to all these waste products inside the closed system of a spaceship? If they were allowed to build up, the air would soon be too foul to breathe, and the stacked-up bags of urine and feces would eventually fill up the spaceship.

The spaceships that have been used in flights around the earth and to the Moon have been equipped with efficient air-purifying systems. The air in the spaceship cabin is pumped over and over again through filters, absorbers, and other devices, to remove the excess carbon dioxide, water vapor, and other wastes and keep the air breathable. But on the short trips, that have been taken so far, not much has been done about recycling other body wastes. They have usually been dumped out of the hatch.

Yet on a long flight, body wastes could be a valuable "natural resource." Methods have already been developed to remove the dissolved chemicals from urine, leaving pure water that can be used for various purposes—even drinking. Solid wastes, after treatment to kill bacteria, could be used as fertilizer for the spaceship's "gardens"— vegetables and other plants grown on beds of sand, to which water and nutrients are added. These plants, and perhaps some tanks of algae and other single-celled forms, would have two functions: as a food source, and to help keep the gases of the air in balance by taking in carbon dioxide and giving off oxygen. The waste products of the astronauts' bodies could thus be reused, over and over again, in the closed system of the spaceship.

Today, some scientists believe that we should start thinking of our whole planet as a closed system. They say that our "Spaceship Earth" will be in serious trouble soon, if we do not learn to recycle our wastes instead of just dumping them into our air and water. Some of the wastes that are now polluting our planet are products of industry. But some are the wastes of our own bodies. With all the talk about phosphates in detergents, for example, the phosphorus in our own feces probably contributes more to the pollution of lakes and

69

streams. Gradually, better methods of treating sewage and recycling waste products are being developed. The "excreta" of our modern society may become valuable natural resources instead of pollution problems, if only we learn in time to reuse them wisely.

INDEX